Superstructural Berlin

A Superstructural Tourist Guide to Berlin
for the Visitor and the New Resident

First published by Zero Books, 2015
Zero Books is an imprint of John Hunt Publishing Ltd., Laurel House, Station Approach,
Alresford, Hants, SO24 9JH, UK
office1@jhpbooks.net
www.johnhuntpublishing.com
www.zero-books.net

For distributor details and how to order please visit the 'Ordering' section on our website.

Text copyright: Nicolas Hausdorf 2014

ISBN: 978 1 78535 065 8
Library of Congress Control Number: 2015932356

A CIP catalogue record for this book is available from the British Library.

Design: Alexander Goller

Printed and bound by CPI Group (UK) Ltd, Croydon, CR0 4YY, UK

We operate a distinctive and ethical publishing philosophy in all
areas of our business, from our global network of authors to
production and worldwide distribution.

Superstructural Berlin

A Superstructural Tourist Guide to Berlin
for the Visitor and the New Resident

Nicolas Hausdorf

Designed by Alexander Goller

Winchester, UK
Washington, USA

CONTENTS

»

written by **Nicolas Hausdorf**
designed by **Alexander Goller**

SPECIAL THANKS TO

Theodore Price,
Jennifer Schmitt,
Resa Mohabbat-Kar,
Robert Lee Best III,
Bianca Lyla Clifford

"A new class: polytoxicomane and health-conscious, multi-sexual, supracultural"

Airen – Strobo

"Thus the metropolitan type of man – which, of course, exists in a thousand individual variants – develops an organ protecting him against the threatening currents and discrepancies of his external environment which would uproot him. He reacts with his head instead of his heart. In this an increased awareness assumes the psychic prerogative. Metropolitan life, thus, underlies a heightened awareness and a predominance of intelligence in metropolitan man. The reaction to metropolitan phenomena is shifted to that organ which is least sensitive and quite remote from the depth of the personality. Intellectuality is thus seen to preserve subjective life against the overwhelming power of metropolitan life, and intellectuality branches out in many directions and is integrated with numerous discrete phenomena."

Georg Simmel – The Metropolis and Mental Life

"The eyes have been used to signify a perverse capacity — honed to perfection in the history of science tied to militarism, capitalism, colonialism, and male supremacy — to distance the knowing subject from everybody and everything in the interests of unfettered power. The instruments of visualization in multi-nationalist, postmodernist culture have compounded these meanings of disembodiment. The visualizing technologies are without apparent limit. The eye of any ordinary primate like us can be endlessly enhanced by sonography systems, magnetic resonance imaging, artificial intelligence-linked graphic manipulation systems, scanning electron microscopes, computed tomography scanners, color-enhancement techniques, satellite surveillance systems, home and office video display terminals, cameras for every purpose from filming the mucous membrane lining the gut cavity of a marine worm living in the vent gases on a fault between continental plates to mapping a planetary hemisphere elsewhere in the solar system. Vision in this technological feast becomes unregulated gluttony; all seems not just mythically about the god trick of seeing everything from nowhere, but to have put the myth into ordinary practice. And like the god trick, this eye fucks the world to make techno-monsters"

Donna Haraway – Situated Knowledges: the Science Question in Feminism and the Privilege of Partial Perspective

"Our eyes fuck the world,
and we're out to fuck"
The authors

Sociology [səʊsiˈɒlədʒi]:
blackmagical masculine form of clairvoyance / sorcery

AVANT-PROPOS

See for example the
development of the
Smart City

This work is an incomplete *essai* that tries to extract
and describe some of the material structure of the
inertia of expectation we have come to refer to
as *society*. It is an attempt to figure out where we
are heading in the development of twenty-first
century living systems. As True urbanites, as Simmel
suggests, we need to develop heightened senses
and start mapping our urban surroundings, which
have long lost their innocence for us in times of
increasingly immersive feedback devices* rendering
macro- and micro-manageable the mechanisms of
social control. This is therefore a first attempt in
the construction of a theoretical weapon, a low-fi-
subjective tool which has been rendered transparent
for all attempts of open-source theoretical
engineering. Primarily built as a polemical cultural
meme and cognitive device, it is also a call to arms
for the re-appropriation of the city to all those
conscious of their historical responsibility.

This *essai* must also be every decent sociologist's
methodological nightmare circumventing / short-
circuiting all elaborate customs and rituals of
remodeling sociology, according to twenty-first
century "scientific" methods which we believe are
rendering it the impotent and toothless adjunct of
the *pensée unique*. We hold against this an analysis
which is all subjective experience, a product of
innumerable observations, directed by an assembly
of overgrown obscured politico-theoretical
background-software ignorantly pursuing the sex-
and death-drive of cognitive mapping and pattern
recognition.

PROLOGUE

ACT ONE

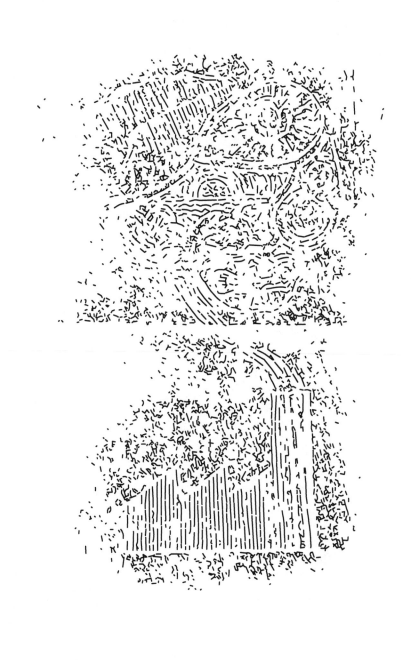

CALL OF THE METROPOLIS

Berlin, Berlin, Berlin: the body may have already
departed but a fraction of the mind always remains
there. Flickering stroboscopic impressions of drug
fueled, opulent weekend nightlife safaris garnished
with chill-outs in the large Hegelian apartments
of the Prussian aristocracy; a backdrop imagery of
socialist fantasy and cold war magnetism.

With flashback images a powerful myth expands
spore-like throughout capitals European and abroad,
soon into the quiet desperation of globalistan's
hinterlands.

("BERLIN")

Subsequent influx of young creatives from all
over, mass-exodus from the slow dread of rotting
provinces and the machinist high-speed insanity of
world capitals, destination TXL, SXF:

(They say:)

A 1980s New York / a dystopian dream-space
melting pot / a virgin creative laboratory / a
bunker-laced postindustrial wasteland waiting to be
refurbished / a hybrid of liberal metropolis and free
space for all alternative lifestyles and idiosyncrasies /

Berlin's imaginary: young, fast and romantic,
Wings of Desire. Condemned to becoming.

We may wonder whether there isn't something
truly *contemporary* about this appeal. How else could
we explain those masses of young people seeking
exile in reunited Germany's born again capital? Is
Berlin the model city for post-industrialism, post-
socialism, post-nationalism? Although the iron cage
of capitalist modernity is clearly perceptible here,
it seems softer than elsewhere, not as brutal: As if a
gentle cloak was slowing down the ravaging speed
of capital and reuniting those wishing to resist the
hyper-speed hubs of the new West. What is the
meaning of this historical occurrence? We must
delve deeper into the structure of this metropolis.

6

THEORETICAL ARMOURY:
SUPERSTRUCTURE AND URBAN SYNTAX

Super-structure: Marxist lingo covered in late 1960s
library dust. Of course there must be a reason why
Karl Marx and later Antonio Gramsci devoted some
energy to the term. They perceived a significant
value of their social analysis in designating a
description of something akin to, well, *mass
consciousness*. After all, this consciousness is both the
basis and the constant product of social relations,
and it may present us with a way to understand,
observe, and encase in a sterile conceptual laboratory
the *normality* of the present. This work could
have aimed at capturing the *Spirit of Berlin*, but a
suchlike notion may well rather obfuscate both
the particularity as well as the exemplariness of
the city in the context of more global processes.
Superstructure is thus a more interesting term,
precisely because it points to *structure*, the material
conditions of the production of consciousness. After
all, the product of structure and superstructure
constitutes a historical era* as distribution of social
forces: because Berlin consciousness, through the
exchange and flux of individuals, today influences
European consciousness and thereby increasingly
world consciousness.

And because material structure and superstructure
are without a doubt reciprocally influential**, our
gaze must find a prominent platform, a theoretical-

*

Similar to Antonio
Gramsci's notion of the
Historical Bloc (*Blocco
Storico*)

**

We will leave the
tactics regarding
superstructure for both
Marx and Gramsci to
determine.

aesthetical plane which allows us to swerve over the concrete jungle scanning it from above for material manifestations of Berlin 'ideology', 'spirit', or 'lifestyle'.

Let us have a look into this urban theater: already without knowing the specifics, we have an intuitive sense from observing the patterns of similarities in those around us that Berlin must be like a factory producing a very particular type of persona, a *historical subjectivity*. Let us venture through the city and identify the countless signifiers of the large theater of spiritual production which is Berlin.

In this journey, we perceive urban space as an inter-play of infrastructures, like assembly lines they manufacture the spirit of today: the product of the mesh of their interaction is the present. They serve as the cornerstones for the rapid trans-generational psychological transformations which have become emblematic for that bound and borderless contemporary *Empire*; whichever may be its specific legal or cultural geopolitical emanation (the "West", the "European Union", the "Transatlantic Market", the "Global Cities", the "International Community" etc.). Located within Berlin city limits, these infrastructures become veritable *export champions* of consciousness. Now let us please put on our most serious sociologist facial expression and venture on a conceited and detached meta-tour through the metropolis.

THE

OF

IN

INFRA -

ACT TWO

PRODUCTION

BERLIN

FIVE

STRUCTURES

**
Concept by Marxist Michel Clouscard who considers the 68 revolutionaries' anti-authoritarianism to have been a Trojan Horse for the introduction of a neoliberalism structured by desire into all domains of life. Consumerism in this way has replaced public morals and politics. See: Néofascisme et idéologie du désir (1972)

SCENERY

Berlin, hyperborean drug capital. Fresh omnipresent scent of heavy marijuana-spice turning entropic in its summertime alleys, exhausted battery-acid cut amphetamine sweat drips from camouflaged nightclub ceilings. Toxic alcoholic aura of workers and desperados on the morning U-Bahn* while Tanatos- teens and poets still celebrate morbid *Zoo Station* imaginary and shoot Heroin to the drone of Bowie's Heroes.

Berlin is a vivid marketplace of pharmacological alchemy offering alternatively doses of empathy and happiness (Ecstasy, MDMA), various states of sedation (Marijuana, Hashish), agitation (Speed, Crystal-Methamphetamine, and Cocaine), fragmentation ((LSD, LSA, and mushrooms) and dissociation (Ketamine, Heroin). A drug culture ubiquitous as it is almost inescapable for any newcomer.

Soon it dawns upon this new resident that Berlin's society is heavily subsidized by a vanity-case of drugs providing the flipside to its traditional background of rigorous protestant Prussian ethics and frugality. Of course, drugs produce a particular historical subjectivity, which is also highly functional in administering initiation-mechanisms to contemporary *liberal-libertarian*** societies. Now please ingest your poison of choice and embark on a psychoactive stroll with us through this murky substance swamp drama.

PRODUCTION

Fragmentations

Drugs are highly differentiated and functional psychological and social devices. They are responsible for a specific production of subjectivity by intervening in the lifestyles and identities of consumers in multiple ways, ranging between processes of fragmentation, alienation and identification. The young consumer - far from inexperienced with drug use - is in reality not only already heavily familiar with the use and culture of mind altering consumption patterns (sugar, television, video games, caffeine, alcohol etc.), she has also been continuously familiarized with the concept of drugs through a cultural industry which has pitched and catered the substances to her from an early age.

Especially today's largely trans-nationalized popular culture could be perceived as having abandoned all of its 1980s moral pretensions of ambiguity or undesirability of drug use. Drugs may well be portrayed as destructive devices; they are de-facto linked to some of the most highly aestheticized cultural commodities. A crass divergence of highly capitalized private sector drug aestheticization competes with toothless public anti-drug campaigns which reek of *state*, *boredom*, and *square stagnation*. They, atavisms of long lost social models, provide no match for the consumerist rituals of permissive society which demand transgression, creativity, and rebellion from the younger generations in order to break the socio-ideological bonds attaching them to the older generations.

*

The rebel ("without a cause") persona is itself a product of the cultural industry aiming to expand its mass commodity market in the 1950s with the help of adolescents' undeveloped pre-frontal cortices.

**

Of course every generation, class and social milieu has its own drug films and mythologies (from Easy Rider, Scarface to Half Baked)

***

(1981) Uli Edel

****

(2008) Hannes Stöhr

Especially in a society which is based upon the constant ritual of transgression (which is the ritual of adolescence *par excellence*) the moral admonishments of anti-drug campaigning provide no match against highly stylized personality models like the rebellious* hip hop hustler, the romantic grunge head, the in-style cynical yuppie, the polytoxic underground artist or the YSL drug corpse walking the catwalk high, dead, and *super vogue*. Omnipresent Hollywood adores drugs, advertising all substances through its frenetic celebrities replaying the Polaroid drama of occult / morbid personality dissolution, from Marilyn Monroe to Miley Cyrus: in its music video party lifestyle or some of its most alluring films (From *American Psycho* (Cocaine, Halcion, Xanax, Ecstasy), *Enter the Void* (Cocaine, LSD, GHB, DMT), to Kids (Marijuana, MDMA), *Nowhere* (MDMA, Amphetamines, Marijuana) or *Naked Lunch* (Heroin, Bug-powder) and, *Requiem for a Dream* (Heroin, Amphetamines))**.

Now watch your step around the cinema fire exits, for among the ticket stubs lurk dirty needles. Of course, drug culture through the trans-nationalization of youth culture escapes confinement in a localizable space. Nonetheless, Berlin has managed to produce a specific local imaginary, cognitively attaching its streets to global drug culture through works like *"Christiane F."****(Heroin), or the more contemporary *"Berlin Calling"*****(MDMA, Ketamine), eternally linking the city to romanticized loci of consumption. Regardless, lured by the magic attraction of drug aestheticism, the young city-dweller therefore heads for the ultimate adventure in the society of control. The escape to Berlin as the seemingly last rebellion against meticulously preplanned normativity initiates a process that will *facilitate* socialization into contemporary reality in a different and complementary way: In creeping *narco-alienation*, the user starts dissociating from the symbols of authority. By way of drug use, he enters into a permanent mild illegality, depriving him of his full capacity and legality of a citizen through the inability to uprightly confront the forces of law and order whose power is permanently rendered visible and enhanced due to the illegality of his drug use. A permanent friction results from harassing the user on his way to the park and from the club. Induced by the fear of prosecution, the police furthermore begin to serve as the primary identification focus of his enmity, despite arguably being much closer to him socially than the real concentrations of political power. A wide variety of versions of "ACAB", "Fuck the Police" are common memes inscribed into city minds and surface. Drugs as a culturally divisive mechanism thereby introduce a separation between forces of order and citizenry, postulating the police as the enemy and thereby rendering them into alienated agents of repressive government*. This culture of separation finds its microcosmic expression in Berlin's regular May 1st clashes: a sclerotic and ritualized expression of the least subversive of anti-state contestations**, which finds its complement in the bathrooms of bars and restaurants overflowing with the sticker-signifiers of Antifa***- and Black-Block promoted anti-nationalism, anti-Germanism, and anti-statism. The antagonism towards the police and a set of

*
A decisive process in which the systematically induced paranoia as internal organization mechanism for the forces of order, often recruited from the "hard-working" social classes and already resentful of the student leisure class drug consumer, is facilitated.

**
Experience has rendered rather evident that the sensibilities of the working classes have never shown much sympathy with street rioting and property damage.

***
Perhaps unsurprisingly, tracing the streams of financing for the Antifa, Germany's network of anti-fascist organizations one finds at the end of the chain... the state itself.

⟶

'Berlin's Weed infrastructures'
A complex network of legal- geopolitical- and sociological trajectories are at the origin of the users daily dose of soma.

laws prohibiting this lifestyle reinforce the drug user's identification with the drug-commodity rebellion. It becomes the possibility of supremely independent socialization and challenge of order, a traditional theme serving the instincts of youth and adolescence ("take a hit from the joint and you're a rebel")*.While she believes to rebel against the status quo, the initiate's emerging drug lifestyle increasingly functions as a full identification with contemporary imperial organization of space (transnational, permissive, consumerist, extra-legal, propped up by violent networks).

Spirituality becomes replaced with a consumable psychoactive hedonism (*Soma*) deeply pervading Berlin's social fabric from the Parliament member to the construction worker. The consequence of this model of regularization and integration of drug use into social life is the normalization of prosthetic substance for well-being, a function which will smoothly and in a gradual transition be continued by the pharmaceutical cartels and the commodity industry. This logic finds its intellectual expression in the fashionable and culturally increasingly omnipresent theories of trans-humanism of the "new left" ("gender", "cyborg"**). The theories advocating full control over emotional and physical capacities as ideals to be striven for***, meanwhile always remain in line with the new world's techno-optimism in their declaration of an unlimited alterability and transcendence of the human body, which becomes a mere attachment port or interface for technology****.

*
A logic which seems all the more dubious if one takes into account how drugs have broken social movements from the '68 rebellion, to the Black Panthers, or Chinese resistance to British imperialism.

**
And at the end of the chain recuperated by industrialized pop stars like Lady Gaga.

***
A logic perhaps finding its true expression less in a utopian equality than in the coked up manager and the single childless woman on antidepressants working until burn-out and placing the interests of the hierarchy above the bodies they have learned to abstract and to commodify.

****
The same logic consequently makes the human being entirely obsolete, in the long run.

*

The aesthetics
of relativity,
fragmentation, and
prosthetization
are perhaps best
captured by Norman
Foster's Reichstag or
Chipperfield's Neues
Museum.

Berlin in this regard plays the role of an ideal laboratory space for trans-humanism, supplying the right dosage combination of liberal legislation, substance availability, and metropolitan alienation. Could the city not be considered a monument to post-humanism's unlimited alterability of form, having over time incorporated the most varied ideological adventures and shifted its architecture accordingly? From Prussian grandeur to Eastern collectivism the city has currently settled upon some sort of postmodernist aesthetic consensus, hybridizing the fragments and ruins of the city with the signifiers of financial capitalism*.

The distribution of space in Berlin itself subsidizes drug use and drug culture. Accessible and unmonitored spaces, liberal policies, the occasion of ruins, abandoned, morbid and decaying houses, the abundance of public parks, and what amounts to a 24/7h club culture are the ideal locations for an unperturbedly developing user culture, both in terms of physical and psychological appropriation. The open and unmonitored spaces for example particularly lend themselves to U-Bahn drug dealing, extending a networked U-Bahn drug economy along the vectors of U7 (from U Wilmersdorfer Straße to Hermannplatz), U8 (Hermannstraße to Rosenthaler Platz), and U9 (Leopoldplatz). These lines are the skeleton to a citywide user culture and are providing the depressing aesthetic background of the drug-economy's lumpenproletariat, which is the morphine user on her eternal, mindless and exhausted strife for the next hit. Zombified users like morbid teeth blend into the shiny swarms of hip youth roaming *Kottbusser Tor* and *Hermannplatz*, they stuff to capacity the U-Bahn and sneak into the café-toilets at *Rosenthaler Platz*, listening / overdosing to eternally repeating background audio recordings of Thompson's *"Fear and Loathing in Las Vegas"*, which plays in St. *Oberholz's* sterile 1970s youth hostel-like bathrooms.

————————→
'Drug psycho-geography'
Berlin's heroin infrastructure, the drug-lines U7, U8 and U9, is only the logistical distribution hub of a century of cultural programming.

PRODUCTION

Pledge of Allegiance

The use of drugs also serves as a subtle identification mechanism of the user to the true forces governing his society, always heavily linked to the security services and mafias involved in the large scale drug trafficking from Afghanistan (via Kosovo) and South America (via Guinea Bissau and Liberia). Those criminal cartels are de facto working hand in hand with high finance and the secret services through money laundering and irregular warfare financing*.

Identification with the shady topology, aesthetic, and parallel society of covert drug use therefore also becomes identification with those secret executive branches of the transnational ruling class. On a more societal level, sympathy with the archetype libertarian drug dealer is sympathy with the ruthless entrepreneur of capitalism. Isn't he after all the most obvious emanation of the pursuit of rational self-interest and minimum taxation of his labor**?

This type of internationalization and similarity of an emerging drug culture with globalization becomes best illustrated through the microcosm of the public parks *Hasenheide* and *Görlitzer Park* or the *RAW Gelände* area.

Here we can find the economic basis of a vast shadow-economy fueled by the misery of refugees as the ground level distribution agents of city-wide somatization. Especially in *Görlitzer Park*, a staff of

*
Information of such links can be found in the instructive *Iran Contra Affair* and its various antecedents and aftermath detailed in works such as *Alfred McCoy* (2003) - *The Politics of Heroin, Gary Webb* (1999) - *Dark Alliance, Peter Dale Scott* (2014) - *American War Machine.*

**
It comes as no surprise that contemporary series such as *Breaking Bad* become instant successes, gambling on the viewer's sympathy with the drug dealer who in reality destroys and alienates their social relations. Instead the viewer becomes complicit in the personal-split by rejoicing in the punishment and destruction of the protagonist's law abiding and integer personality side, which the character in the series progressively abandons.

*

Coke-heads

**

Couldn't the complicity
of the state be any
better highlighted
than by pointing at the
contradictions of times,
where an increasingly
total global
surveillance grid does
not stand in opposition
to an increasingly
abundant supply of
somata and organized
transnational criminal
structures?

up to 150 dealers is operating under the nimbus
of gigantic rooftop-sized graffiti spelling *"MDMA"*
and *"Kokserinnen*"*, as if advertising the operations
of an ever increasing supply of crypto head-of-
sales becoming initiated into the semiotics of the
globalized drug economy.

Their chains to a semi-legal status, the responsibility
to sustain families living abroad, and payments
for transfer debts to Mafiosi organizations,
meanwhile ensure their forceful socialization into
criminal labor and guarantee the installation of a
permanent future *tiersmondized* lumpenproletariat
in the first world. They also form the particular
subterranean structure of organized crime in the
network society whose origins are certainly never
thoroughly investigated by the police forces. The
latter, bowing down to political pressure on the
top-levels, contend themselves with constant
crackdowns and surveillance missions on the street
- and, every once in a while reaching the medium-
supply level (obliged by popular sentiment), without
ever really investigating the systematic drug cartel
based imports on a global level**. Berlin subculture
meanwhile recuperates this cultural meme and
criminal economy under the guise of social
liberalism and "tolerance" towards narcotics and
its pushy agents. Hedonism supports the structures
both ideologically and financially, accepting the
continuing semi-legal exploitation and introduction
of a refugee labor force into an expanding shadow
economy, which in the long run perpetuates
the subversion of society by organized criminal
networks. As for the on-the-ground distributing

agents themselves, they are certain to be the first ones to be turned into public scapegoats (in the logic of deprivation / overcompensation) should the public's anger about omnipresent drug sales boil over. Liberal-libertarianism then turns into its securitarian janus-face.

$\longrightarrow$

'Essai of a Polytoxic topology'

SCENERY

hypnotic initiation and tabula rasa of a Berlin weekend. Immersive architectures organized as a network of cultic infrastructures are proliferating the dark and deep whispers of machine language-Techno, Electro, Minimal, Dubstep, Trance, and Goa. No explanation possible for Berlin's contemporary success without its night-club networks: the city lives through nurturing itself from its all week-long nightlife. Bearing the advantage of no legally imposed closing hour for nightclubs, parties may occasionally run on from Thursdays straight through to Mondays without a break. Opening and closing parties of *scene* places continue for a week without end. In opposition to the regular twenty-first century economy capital that explodes its offices into short eruptions of after work binge-drinking, Berlin residents have turned partying into dedicated day-long feasts. Nightlife is an expertly practiced past-time, lived with seriousness and devotion. It may commence at 2 o'clock at night and evolve into a 30 to 48 hour odyssey throughout a variety of venues, ranging from polished cocktail bars to obscure night and swinger clubs, sleazy Kebab joints, ostentatious confectionaries, hotel saunas and swimming pools: eclectic dérives, cradles of city-psychosphere, highly subsidized by the city's makeshift stagnating economy, abundant space, liberal government and rampant hedonism. Berlin in this regard marks the emergence of a popularization of the traditionally elitist leisure class relatively freed from the shackles of economic overexploitation and therefore capable of extending *partying* into a sustainable life-style model.

PRODUCTION

Initiations for a New Citizenry

Almost as if by instinct one apperceives Berlin's nightclubs as production hubs. Often set against backgrounds of industrial atrophy (*Kater Holzig, Bar 25, Sisiphos*) or themselves hosted in abandoned power plants (*Berghain*, the late *Tresor*), the nightclub economy marks the shift in the transformation of Berlin from a hub of commodity production into a hub of postindustrial personality manufacturing, as well as the shift from the industrial economy to the sign economy. The undead spirits of Berlin's long lost manufacturing facilities resurface in telluric rituals as hypnotic rhythms taking possessions of the uninscribed youth flocking into the city. In Germany, the industrial production capital of Europe, the sound of the machine reigns supreme and is spread to the imperial periphery.

Berlin's club infrastructure is the network infrastructure operating this magical transformation. It has become a true initiation-rite to the city for a new Berliner to commit to a three day uninterrupted drug fueled pilgrimage from one club to another, with the only goal of a satisfying final exhaustion. On one's way, one will inevitably be introduced to a number of themes central to contemporary subjectivity: clubs are the locations where a banalization of transgression is operated at a subcultural level. Clubs observe a strict code of supra-nationalism and gender equality. Steamy drug fueled polygamy and non-conventional sexual encounters in unisex toilets interlaced with visits to

It is interesting to note
that the party drugs
LSD and Ketamine
are similarly classics
of early mind control
and reprogramming
experiments such as
MK Ultra.

**

See Chapter 4

a vampiresque dance floor blasé and cool do not
allow for a continuation of "traditional" value
systems. It is here that normativity (the "nation", the
"family", and "morality") is being shattered and
recreated as trans-nationalist capitalist subjectivity
to atonal beats, chopped up in psychoactive
transitions by the dj controlling the mass body.
Subliminal meta-narratives of freedom and youth
through consumption and "letting go" are conveyed
through *Function One* speakers directly and highly
immersively into the brains of the night-life citizen.
Club infrastructure operates as a network of cultural
hypnosis, slowly but securely infusing a precise set of
values and aesthetics into the cultural-multiplier
popular-body, slowly but securely reprogramming
Berlin's youth*. Cold electronic baselines fuse with
heartbeats, predetermining a safe-frame emotional
spectrum and industrial clockwork of the city. Clubs,
of course, are also structures of distribution,
consumption of narcotics and interface with the
psycho-cultural programming of adolescent pop-
culture (see Chapter 1).

The magnetic attraction of the music is similarly the
consumer citizen's allegiance and familiarity with
technological morbidity and meditative indifference.
Pale dance-floor citizens trance-form into the
stoic atomized subjects of post-industrialism:
controlled, centralized and outsourced releases
of oxytocin via MDMA create the temporary
networked communities, and leave behind the
borderline- personality sensitivity of disrupted
neurotransmitters indispensable for the productive
patterns of the creative classes and motor for the
sign economy**.

Part of the inauguration of the dance floor citizen to Berlin is the calculated code, obscure and indiscernible to the uninitiated observer, yet crucial for status in the postindustrial exchange relations of semio-capitalism. Primary point of operation of the *code* are the queues (segregation lines) forming before the nightclub entrances.

The bouncer becomes the primary agent and connoisseur of cool, rejecting the overly excited tourist as well as the culturally illiterate, whose initial rejection will only push them deeper into a consuming desire of knowledge of *the code*. The controller-watcher breaks up the herd and forms the individual liable to judgment for his efforts in distinction.

It is here that one can identify the subtle incorporation of cultural rituals, in a city never overdressed but with a precisely and rationally calculated cool-commodity, which is strictly observed, managed and passed on by the rule of the bouncers guarding the entrance. Only the true observer of these codes will, for example, continuously enter into the most exclusive nightclubs: an eternal scenic limbo where crowds ranging from international chic to middle class hedonist homosexuals mingle.

Religious silence, suppressed excitement, and sheepish obedience will accompany the long queue into the club, where the moods and personal gustos of the bouncers reign supreme over willing subjects anxious to be accepted. It is here also that an ideological selection takes place, where the

$\longrightarrow$

'Cultural fracking'
The most immersive in the shortest possible time span: Berlin's club infrastructure is the jack-hammer to 19th century models of social organization.

subject is faced with the limits of individuality: the bouncer becomes the objective instance, judging upon the conformity with the code. Whereas similar mechanisms of selection operate in many cities, their prominence in Berlin has made them an obsession unmatched by any capital. Only Berlin with its popularized leisure class and reduced prominence and availability of regular capitalist status symbols has made the code a truly democratic concern. A prominence, which can also best be expressed through the becoming-legend of photographer Sven Marquardt Berghain's stylish tattooed face bouncer, by now a cultural icon of city-wide prestige. A large scale mural by Portuguese street artist Vhils can be found at *Potsdamer Straße* immortalizing the portrait of the selection agent, as if supplying the contemporary and corporate funded* equivalent to socialist iconography: self-made men virtuous by merit are operating selection**.

The central status of partying in the cultural system can similarly be found in the aesthetics of Berlin clubs itself, where even after years of capitalization an almost egalitarian promise reigns that supports understatement and punishes too overt displays of wealth. Immersive environments, drug and sexual consumerism temporarily blind out class, race and gender structures. One nation under pleasure. Mass produced consciousness and a subtle conformity in appearance are produced at waiting lines and guest lists, transfigured by an immense proliferation of mythical discourses on how to get 'in' - accepted into the wombs of the most selective clubs and past their kafkaesque justice.

*

Vhils was sponsored by a popular jeans manufacturer.

**

The pop-cultural equivalent of the bouncer is the jury of the omnipresent casting shows.

Obedience, code, selection: in the end, club culture
is only mirroring the liberal workspace and
the social models of exclusion, which of course
almost instinctively also makes clubs notorious
infrastructures of drug distribution. The clubbers'
reward for obedience and observance of the code
(loyalty to the sign economy) is pleasure. The price
is his transgression and adherence to transgressive
social liberalism. This liberalism may certainly
take different forms depending on time and place,
ranging from the softer *culturo-chichi* crowd of the
exclusive *China Club* - or the polished *Felix Club*,
Watergate, *Weekend*, or *Cookies*, where the aspiring
middle classes mix with the established, to enjoy
polished drinks, mild-mannered music and pleasant
views.

More radically hedonistic venues include *Sisyphos*,
Kosmonaut and *Kater Blau**, all in the legacy of
legendary *Bar 25*, and are marked by a makeshift
aesthetic of wooden, fair-like structures, festival
and camping site-like chill outs and all day outdoor
sessions in the summer. Another example is *Salon zur
Wilden Renate*, a former apartment blog successively
turned into an adolescent fantasy, with a circus-like
interior and even a labyrinth that can be visited
during the daytime.

Berghain, the most internationally renowned club in
this mix, certainly occupies a specific rank in Berlin's
cultic infrastructure. An emblematic brutal structure
and silhouette thrown into empty post death-strip
borderland desert, *Berghain* has become a strategic
hub for the proliferation of discourses and myth.
A mixture of raw, ascetic radicalism, encased in a
vast temple-like structure with massive columns,

free-floating staircases and what appears, at least
from the hovering staircase leading to *Panorama
Bar*, to be a greenish bathtub of crawling insectoid
party-goers: A distinct smell of pheromones, leather,
anal penetration and acidic amphetamine roams
throughout darkrooms and unisex toilets, which
are mere prison-like cold metal bowls under dimly
lit metal grilled ceilings. With strategically placed
fierce looks, visitors are reminded at the door
that photographs are forbidden inside in order to
maintain anonymity for the possibility of tasteful
debauchery, while similarly aiding the production
and sustainability of the myth emanating from this
former industrial space.

While distinctively counter-cultural in appearance –
a staircase leading to *Panorama Bar* is lined with the
photography of Sven Marquardt glorifying Berlin's
pretension to egalitarianism with its central subject –
the supposed social outcast*, rather counter*intuitively*
–, the place is subtly hybridized with a corporate
smoking lounge sponsored by big tobacco, precisely
hinting at the amalgamate of social and economic
agendas which is liberal-libertarian rule.

Despite its gritty appearance, *Berghain*, due to its
restrictive door policy, minimalist aesthetics and
hypnotic immersive environment, has become an
emblematic hangout for Berlin's aspiring cultural
elite-a hub for an immaterial currency and a central
bank of cultural semiotics, where only those who
have perfectly incorporated the sub-cultural codes
are continuously safe from rejection. The club has
become the reference point for a decentralized
network of club culture which is producing,
transforming, and exporting European avant-
gardist subjectivity via Berlin.

*
One may ask whether
the homosexual /
queer / outcast has not
precisely become the
mainstream in Berlin.

⟶

'Aftermath of the
weekend-dérive'
*Invisible softwares are
structuring this trajectory*

I

SCENERY

(Nightly conversation outside of a night-club)

"So what do you do?"
"I'm an ARTIST..."

Berlin: new promised land for the international arts. The sector's signifiers proliferate exuberantly throughout city surface texture: street art is effervescing over Wilhelminian style facade, androgynous crowds enveloped in fleeting seam float through grim downtowns softening rough neighbourhood *edge*, galleries / alien-commodity merchants pop up near money-laundry kebab stands conveying cryptic concepts born in international universities in soft and exotic accents. The impact of a continuous stream of German and international artists finding their home in Berlin, as steady as the exodus of reputed galleries to the capital, has become increasingly noticeable as a mainstream movement in recent years. The movement has thereby also become an economic phenomenon of non-negligible proportion and world-wide reputation. After all, Berlin galleries by now constitute 34 of 300 participants at the prestigious and capital soaked *Art Basel*, a litmus test for the competitiveness of cities in the sector. Of course, less explored is the way in which the network that is constituted by all things *art* has by now inevitably become a major factor in the production of contemporary subjectivity. Let us therefore grab our free cheap *vernissage* wine and *hors d'oeuvre* and take a stroll together around this urban exhibit.

PRODUCTION

Occupied Territories

It has become a banality to point out gentrification in cities and the role that artists have played in the processes of urban cleansing ("stormtroopers of gentrification"). Every major city has by now learned the strategy of attracting an artistic crowd to a specific geographic area of a city in order to increase real estate value, and in the process cleanse the areas of those populations deemed detrimental to property value. Artists are ideal on-setters of the process through their entrepreneurial spirit and overdeveloped distinction drive which constantly leads them to settle amongst the dulled, apathetic, or impoverished local populations they deem the markers of the "real". In reality, they thereby always commence the displacement of populations according to income, and increasingly create the impulses for the social Darwinist organization of space in the twenty-first century with its increasingly separated center-periphery relationships.

This process, certainly, is far from being unique to Berlin, while the extent and specifics of the process make it worth taking a more detailed look. Berlin, when compared to other West-European cities, facilitates the process through low entry costs and masses of centrally located and still affordable space. Berlin's right wing populist political *enfant terrible* Thilo Sarrazin once estimated the capacity of the city at 6-7 million people. With a current population estimated at 3.2 million, this should put the infrastructure of the city into perspective: Berlin becomes a primary hub of settlement for European populations, specifically the impoverished yet highly mobile artistic intelligentsia who are in turn enabled to participate in the transformation of available city space. One of the best examples is the ongoing process of micro-gallerisation of South Neukölln, a constantly shifting and decentralized frontline of urban social transformation processes inexorably advancing southwards.

In combination with the city's generally socially liberal nature and impressive existing art scene, it is these places that are attracting a crowd of international intellectuals disgusted with the deterioration of public discourse in their respective homes elsewhere in the West. Although artistic pretension will remain a primary phantasm sustaining an unproductive lifestyle for their majority, off spaces certainly continue to exist. Admittedly, however, the small independent galleries are more often magically / tragically reproducing the games and strategies of highly capitalized art's aesthetic agenda setting.

PRODUCTION

Transgression Machine

Not only are galleries loci of socio-spatial practices, they are also subtly functioning ideological hubs, a networked super-infrastructure advancing the incorporation of new attitudes and values in urban residents, notably the values of liberal-libertarian society. Since the legacy of twentieth century art, ever since Duchamp, has mainly been based upon the theme of transgression, artistic practices *in toto* have come to function as a transgression machine, a sort of anti-Leviathan always in the service of the destruction and inversion of traditional normativity (heterosexuality, family, Catholicism, the nation) and the destruction of taboo. Inexorably, the practices convey a steady canon of attitudes and lifestyles to the urban citizen who is partial to the arts.

The deracinated petit-, to bourgeois urbanite art consumer apprehends a potpourri of seemingly elite ideological practices from the obscure talmudist scholastics of Derrida to Deleuzian legacy philosophies and post-humanist themes (in the legacy of *Orlan, Stelarc*), complemented by a gusto for styles following the trajectory of abstract expressionism: all are operating a targeted fragmentation of the Western enlightenment legacy of logics in favor of an impressionist associative operation of the brain (the figure of the rhizome*). Here the sons and daughters of Europe's social contract congregate to incorporate a relativist obscurantist poetry converging in a variety of practices of aestheticized individualism. Art, as ideological practice, becomes originally appropriated in the gallery openings, obligatory events for the urban in-crowds, and transforms into an increasingly sophisticated array of aesthetic everyday practices, from musical taste to interior design and photography, according to which citizens constantly rebrand themselves and thereby determine their social rank in the leisure class**.

*

Neuroplastic mass-operation heralded by Deleuze and Guattari complemented by the emotional news value logic of private media.

**

Social networks have become primary instruments for this layering of social rank and linked aesthetic consciousness.

*

Journalist precariousness has both its producers and editors well conscious of not biting the (corporate) hand that feeds. For a more historically direct precedent of influence see the legacy of secret service media-interference operations such as Operation MOCKINGBIRD.

**

The elitist practice of art criticism is further reinforced through its monopolization by a range of corporate media.

***

See for example Frances Stonor Saunders "Who Paid the Piper?: CIA and the Cultural Cold War".

****

Of course movements like "l'art pour l'art" or "dandyism" having become completely detoured from political escape strategies to an excuse for an oftentimes empty and meaningless aestheticism.

Ideological coherence in this machine is ensured at a distance through the operations of capital. Targeted placements of financial capital, big corporate sponsorship, state scholarships and foundations paired with opinion leader journalism* ensure the right (in the sense of harmless for the political, financial establishment) development of mass tastes and practices. The network of publicly and privately financed galleries, foundations, and universities work together to produce a congruent meta-narrative guided by the often-times hyper-centralized** damage control and promotion of cultural opinion leaders: a procedure best illustrated by the ongoing preference and success of abstract expressionism over figurative works ever since the end of WWII. The style had been promoted by the CIA as part of its postwar cultural agenda in order to shift art away from more politicized and often anticapitalist themes***.

Historical precedents similarly illustrate how state and financial capital have continuously favored trends convenient to their own survival, ranging from mildly politicized criticisms to purely aesthetic**** works. These in turn become objects of speculation fueled by the similarly virtual and intangible value of high finance as its major financier.

Moneyed collectors eager to find safe and profitable havens for their capital in times of financial disintegration travel to Berlin to sustain personal relations to the artists. Symbiosis is profitable to both, since both rely on the stabilization of the hyper-virtual value of the artworks subject to historical volatility according to changing ideological eras. Visitors to the city, in order to meet the artists, dine distinctly German style with heavy-luxury tracked-heritage meats on white table cloth at *Grill Royal* and *Pauly Saal*. They sip select cocktails at *Bar Tausend* and *Viktoria Bar*. Here those investors desirous to meet face-to-face with the practicing artists whose mystique must guarantee the sustainability and longevity of their investment, can take a relaxing break from the city's blatant remnants of egalitarianism still enshrined in its socialist architecture and its distinct lack of service mentality. In this way, the aging artist who originally moved to Berlin to find an off-space and off-capitalist base for production can slowly be rendered suave and become accommodated to the magical dedication and transformations of capital. Be his works rather mediocre, placed into the enormous dimensions of a Berlin gallery space staffed with the fashionable and conceited *servi culti* of the sector, they will nonetheless strike the observer of being of a particularly majestic quality.

It is this mixture of highly capitalized art, gentrification, and brain-drain towards abandoned city territories that are producing the everyday environments of contradiction that are the fuel of the restless capitalist spirit once so endearing and inspiring to Marx. The area around *Potsdamer Straße* is only one example of how the art market produces its social and aesthetic contradictions, having turned the building abandoned by the *Tagesspiegel*, one of Berlin's mainstream newspapers, into gallery space: *Blain Southern, Thomas Fischer, Figge von Rosen, Tanja Wagner, Tanya Leighton, Sommer & Kohl,*

———————————————→

'The gallery'
Although the gallery undeniably offers a certain range of freedom, it remains constraint by a rigid network of hegemonic ideological, aesthetic, and economic practices.

Isabella Bortolozzi, 401 contemporary, Galerie Helga Maria Klosterfelde, Guido W. Baudach, line up around Potsdamer Straße to deliver an international edge to a part of town still heavily coined by alienated immigration stuffed into social housing projects like Pallas. Together with this vast bunker-like structure housing project which is also home to criminal networks, the galleries are delivering a mini New York-esque vibe to the area, energized by marked social contrasts and contradictions between immigrant youth, veiled women, withered West-Berliners, Arab vegetable salesmen, international art capital and finally, drug-addicted hookers and customers of the sleazy LSD porn-cinema lining Bülowstraße.

Of course, it is not only this grittiness which draws in the artistic class always eager to appreciate the Other, but also the central location of Potsdamer Straße situated a mere 10 minute walk from van der Rohe's Neue Nationalgallerie. Carrying the endearing promise of social success to the city, art soon becomes the collective spiritual project for the modern-day city-dweller, by which he distinguishes himself and intensifies his individuality through processes of self-branding thereby rendering homage to the fact that the control, creation and proliferation of desire is the highest form of contemporary power. Therefore sooner or later, if they do not fall victim to Berlin's at times disconcerting hedonism, most of the young idealistic artists are absorbed either in the established art and gallery scene*, or in the industries of the mind (corporate design, PR) as highly paid marketing employees, with their creative impulses redirected towards the spiritual enslavement and behavioral modification of the masses.

* Such as the makers of ABC contemporary, affectionately known in Berlin as "The Gallery Mafia".

⟶

'Declaration of independence, pt. 2'

SCENERY

Unlimited victorious expansion of co-working spaces, Europe's Silicon Valley ("Silicon Allee"), impenetrable walls of Macbookpro in impossibly trendy coffee-shops, reciprocal mentoring sessions, alternative life-models, spillover of deconstructed working times, Prosecco and *Gründerszene.*

Berlin in the early twenty-first century: an aspiring center of the *New Economy* - that twenty-first century post-industrial promise of continuous growth and unlimited value creation in the sign economy. Post-industrialism however, is not a novel phenomenon to Berlin's economy, and finds its origins in WWII's destruction of two thirds of the city's industrial capacity, perpetuated by corporations leaving the city in consideration of political risks after 1945. Instead, a number of tax benefits soon were flooding both parts of the city with inflated artificial production hubs in an attempt to turn them into ideological showcases for the other side to observe at distance and undermine the moral of the enemy. What followed the (calculated) breakdown of the GDR defining industries, other than leaving the Eastern territories to become mere growth incubators for West German industries, were a range of toothless sectors ranging from entertainment, the creative industries to tourism, some heavy subsidy green economy hubs and the IT sector. Of course, such a novel twenty-first century economic structure must have profound effects on the production of subjectivity.

PRODUCTION

Deindustrialization - Spatial to Spiritual

Of course, de-industrialization must not only be understood as a mere destruction of industries. It is a multi-component social process whose implications are both historical and personal. De-industrialization is firstly due to an increase in efficiency of existing production structures by which formerly industrially employed labor becomes unnecessary for the production process. Jeremy Rifkin, in his 1995 book "The End of Work", already pointed to the obsoleteness of 80% of the population, as production could be assumed by a maximum of 20%. Rifkin was meanwhile far from rejoicing for the masses freed from labor, and anticipated considerable problems for them: the hyper-centralization of production by a few along with the ensuing effects of a hyper-verticalization of power aided by the instruments of international competition and recession, together establish a new relation of power between a newly obsolete labor force and capital with an entirely new dependence of the former upon the latter. Berlin aids this process by preventing and spatially dis-identifying German youth from their social and class origins frequently located in the industrialized German West and South. Instead of demanding a share in the production facilities their parents helped to establish as global enterprises in their home towns, the children of the old social contract generation are drawn into the theme-park of Germany's capital, where they will soon betray their origins for an allegiance to the sign economy of the global hyper-class. They invest their parents'

The collapse of the GDR state had been anticipated by the subversion of East Germany's cognitive sphere by GDR residents watching the broadcasts of West-German state television complemented by intershop supermarkets selling West German products.

**

Ex-Chancellor Helmut Kohl famously predicted "Blühende Landschaften" (prospering landscapes) as the economic future-perspective of the newly integrated GDR territories.

savings into new structures of New Economy immaterial labor production hubs, or bleed the hard labor of the previous generation into the hedonistic infrastructures offered by the city (Chapters 1,2,3).

Of course, industrialization from the viewpoint of capital risks liberating social and political forces with ensuing demands of shorter working hours and more free time. Berlin is therefore experienced as a laboratory for the mixture of social and psychological fragmentation as well as a concomitant disciplining necessary for the reproduction and accentuation of social relations.

PRODUCTION

Inertia / Resignation

After reunification, Berlin's "showcase" industrial subsidy system transformed into a different support system promoting sectors of future economic growth. As a consequence, Berlin's economy crashed against all hopes of becoming the new boom town. Especially the economy of industry-heavy East Berlin after reunification completely disintegrated, initiating a new era of unemployment for many of the city's residents: after a decade-long process of mellowing through the absurdities and dehumanization of the East German bureaucratic dictatorship, as well as aspiration produced by *Westfernsehen* broadcasts* and politician's promises of prospering landscapes**, the residents finally accepted their fate as self-inflicted. This generation still cognitively coins the city: U-and S-Bahn rides

throughout the city oftentimes convey a vibe of
broken biography torn from the slow rot of socialism
and thrown into a new alienating system of
underpaid service labor and complementary social
benefits. Here an air of humiliation and an odour
of alcoholism is balanced out by on-board screens
and commercials aiming to produce the illusion of
an omnipresent petit-bourgeois culture advertising
cheap *Friedrichspalast* Varieté Shows, useless human-
interest news items and aesthetically impaired
commercials.

The lack of a valid economy and purchasing power
can also be observed through the prism of Berlin's
distinct lack of fashion and its disdain for overtly
showy wealth. Flashy attire is scorned in most
parts of the city, while eclectic casual styles from
goa-hippie, to *outdoor-functional-German-province-
all-star* to *3rd-generation-Gastarbeiter-sweatpants* are
dominant styles bewildering *Fashion Week* visitors as
to the city's distinct lack of *urbane.* Further indicators
for lack of purchasing power are the empty and
unused commercial spaces in Berlin's U-Bahn
system: for an absence of commercial customers
they are commonly appropriated by various federal
agencies to promote the dangers of AIDS and the
use of condoms, furthermore creating a cognitive
atmosphere of omnipresent diseased decay where
purchasing power is deemed too low to invest in
advertising by the marketing industry.

Upcoming rushes of energy in Berlin's U-Bahn
system will furthermore be crushed by the casual
obliviousness of most its passengers to the unspoken
metropolitan law of remaining to the right side
of escalators and staircases in order to create a

*
Community by fate /
suffering

**
Or better yet their
non-existence. Up until
1982s Chancellor Kohl
was still considering
sending up to half
of the Gastarbeiters
back to their home
countries, as revealed
by Thatcher-era leaked
secret documents in
2013.

fast track for those in a hurry. At places like the
chronically congested *Hermannplatz*, one can be
sure to always encounter enough destructured
nylon encrusted passengers with an absorbed and
fermenting gaze to completely obstruct the way
to the soon to be departing train. These congested
stairways, while similarly detrimental to the
development of directionality, velocity, and energy
appear as the unlikely counterparts to Berlin's vast
street alley structure, a type of hyper-Haussmannian
anti-revolutionary overcompensation to prevent the
formation of all social interactions / critical masses /
street blockades to come.

Now close your teary, worn, alcohol-swollen eyes
and listen to the somber acoustic of Berlin's syrupy
psycho-sphere: The omnipresent *Berliner Schnauze*
is the local dialect, which appears like an *étude*
of singing resignation. Content-wise, the small
talk celebrates Berlin's *Schicksalsgemeinschaft** by
endlessly repeating the popular themes of rising
prices, the changing of the city for the worse, the
city's stagnation, its corrupt government, or the
eternally bad weather (too cold, too hot, too mild...).
The visitor may be alternatively put off or charmed
by this distinctly frank personality type, which
appears to be impenetrable to the idea of service
mentality (immune system against colonization) and
seems to be constantly punishing curious and good
tempered people. Of course, the distinct mentality
created by a legacy of pain, Prussian disciplinary
punishment and a seemingly decade-old hurt pride
is not restricted to the east of the city. In Neukölln,
the *Arcaden* Shopping Centre presents a bulwark
against gentrification and a monument to decades of
failed German immigration policy**. Here Germany's

multi-generational Gastarbeiter-descendant lumpenproletariat can be observed blandly staring into the scenery while leaning over the railings from the early morning hours on, waiting for the day to pass. A mood of deracination, alienation, and parallel society prevails, watching those begrudgingly gazing upon the wildly dressed international newcomers, which are certain to soon drive them out of their apartments to the drum of rapidly increasing rent-structures.

PRODUCTION

Discipline / Aspiration / Social Control

Certainly, the new economy infrastructure, in order to be effective, also needs to cater to citizens' dreams, desires and aspiration. This is mainly done through a variety of opportunities the city has to offer to the young careerist. Government subsidy and the determined desire to make Berlin Germany's capital have transferred the political sector of the country to the city with all of the industries catering to it: the failed and mediocre lawyers constituting the political sector, the lobbyists working for them loop-holing the common sense once supposed to underlie legislation, and the PR merchants of the mind allow for the manifold possibilities of political parasitism and abandonment of private integrity. The private sector meanwhile offers jobs in the marketing and PR industries, taking advantage of the impulses of the young creatives and artistic class attracted into the city by Berlin's freedom and hedonism (Chapters 1,2,3).

$\longrightarrow$

'**Vassal Economy**'
Successful start ups are sold off to the Valley

A major current meme is the entrepreneurial aspect of the city supposedly embodied in its start-up scene. In a relatively recent development, the low cost of labor and housing mixed with high quality "human capital" is producing the so called "Silicon Allee" culture, where incubator capital is sucking in cheap European talent in order to build tech-start-ups to be grown and consequently spun off to big Silicon Valley capital in case of success: a further step towards an international division of labor with Germany playing a second rank as sub-supplier to the globalized California based tech-giants. Berlin thereby mainly produces online retailers, allowing for a destruction of the small local entrepreneur and his business, further centralizing the economy and bringing it under the *diktat* of transatlantic stock exchange capital.

Entrepreneurs work on the endless commercial space of the Internet with ever new technologies devouring mankind's collective time and promise in order to lock it away on the screen. Meanwhile, the gold rush mentality of the new start up scene is attracting and producing a large number of programmers working to program the "killer app" against rapidly degenerating social skills*. They fill the coffee shops and a new array of trendy co-working spaces from *Betahaus*, with its Thursday morning networking breakfasts to *St.Oberholz, Agora Collective, Wedding's Supermarkt,* and various other new-age looking cafés from Mitte to Kreuzberg to produce Berlin's *"start up culture"*: a favorite talking point of newspapers and increasingly a focal point for the young *arriviste* of international provenance, soon to be appropriated into the

*
Theory of the use of time

———————————→
'**First We took Manhattan...**'

sector's standardized sales and programming jobs. *Tempelhofer Feld*, the vast former airport space forming an urban gap in Southern Neukölln was supposed to constitute the new home for this start up industry, but has been rejected in a popular referendum by a savvy citizenry tired of its rising rent-structure, despite the best efforts of salesmanship by the political class.

The rejection points to a seeming wisdom acquired by the citizenry that the growing shift of economic activity brings them no advantage. To the contrary: the highly specialized and often-times imported workforce will only crowd them out of their living spaces. Meanwhile the largely short-contracted and *flexploited* workers of the sector do not really bring in enough money to become committed and permanent residents. The lack of stability and predictability in these volatile jobs meanwhile adds to the prolonging of non-sedentary lifestyles of employees. Aided by Berlin's hedonistic infrastructures, structural adolescence can finally become *infinite*.

⎯⎯⎯⎯⎯⎯⎯⟶
'Future Shock'

SCENERY

Summer time: 'Easy Jet-set' of all nations floats through Berlin: heavy shopping, committed drugged-out cycling strolls and party marathons are transforming city limits into a permanent hedonist camping site.

Extension of the myth: desire. More than ten million tourists per year wander the streets of Berlin, a steady increase having surpassed all other European cities except for London and Paris. They confer a newly dignified status upon the city and re-approach it to its metropolitan past and legendary status of the roaring 20s. Bewildered and alienated visitors roam the post-human architecture and boredom of *Potsdamer Platz* and its surroundings still haunted by the morbid demon of the border death strip, masses pilgrimage to the evident hyper-real party locations of the amusement park *Friedrichshain*, to the artificial tourist traps from *Hackescher Markt* and *Friedrichsstraße*. A more sophisticated savvy meanwhile arms itself with smartphone apps seeking out the latest hyped joint in *Wedding, Mitte* and *Neukölln* in the perpetual hunt for cool.

Tourism: that particular and constant flux supplying cognitively impressionable conveyor material to the urban syntax. The effects are heavily felt in Berlin: mass tourism is a relatively recent phenomenon for a timid city which had been forcibly turned into an abandoned village by the cold geopolitical constellations reigning supremely and omni-potently over the city until the early 1990s. Tourism is thus both a substance-altering phenomenon as well as a vectorial factor boosting and amplifying all other psycho-active city infrastructures with the fuel of foreign minds and capital.

PRODUCTION

Interzone- Europe's Soma Bin

Of course, Berlin's imaginary is stronger and more peculiar to the visitor than for the permanent resident, and so the tourist produces Berlin as the drug-fueled party paradise she has come to expect. She can act with little inhibitions (the regular logic of tourism), since nobody knows her or could judge her in the indifference and cabals of night-time traffic. Her enthusiasm is the true energy source continuously refueling the myth of Berlin.

Throughout the course of her stay and afterwards, in her interaction with locals as well as friends, Berlin is produced as a steady discourse in which the city is weighed in comparison to other hubs for the international hyper-class.

(They say:)

"Berlin is SO not London", "In Paris I always feel like.., whereas in Berlin", "Berlin is so chilled, empty, ugly, (and so on.)", "Berlin is so unlike the rest of Germany".

It does not matter which respective version of this ever reoccurring conversation one comes across: the interaction itself fulfills the purpose of constantly measuring and weighing Berlin against other cities on the global grid and thereby producing a dynamic of referentiality, competition and ultimately adaptation.

———————→
'Simulacra and...'

The visitor usually loves the city for its slow pace and its parties, while judging it for its provincialism (when compared to New York, London, and Paris), unconscious that these factors are merely two sides of one and the same coin. A lack of capital makes Berlin as comfortable as it makes it at times provincial and square. Berliners on the one hand identify with these discourses and become them, on the other hand they remark the ambiguous processes of gentrification and commodification which put them into competition and thus develop an antibody response in which tourism is denounced for all of its evils. Stickers with the slogans "Fuck you Touri" and "Berlin does not love you" are spread over the patchwork canvasses of bathrooms and U-Bahn stations, reviving the image and deeply embedded WWI & II cultural meme of the hostile German providing the obscene undercurrent to the overly polite, disciplined and perfectly English-speaking internationalized German.

The hedonistic establishment and the local art scene in this way become enmeshed in resistance strategies against outside tourist invasion, while the productive capital represented by the small entrepreneur finds ways to exploit the influx, thereby becoming increasingly aligned to the interest and strategies of financial capital owning real estate and raising prices for rentable space.

The strength of Berlin's myth is assumed by this small entrepreneur willing to deliver the expectation as a readily deliverable and consequently despiritualized mass commodity. Simulacra-copies of successful clubs in the summer-time proliferate around the originals to produce hyper-real party miles. Copies of *Kater Holzig* and *Club der Visionäre* aim at distilling the magic of their concepts and transform the areas around *Schlesisches Tor, Heinrich Heine Straße* and *Watergate* into oftentimes vulgarized copy-cat landscapes aiming to fetch the drunk and drugged masses rejected at the doors of the originals*.

As a consequence, the city becomes polarized: a fragmentation and dynamic sets in rupturing the original social fabric and producing a struggle for the destiny of Berlin, ranging from attempts of an increasingly aggressive preservation of the dream space to its fully assumed exploitation.

In the process of opening-up the city for the exploration of the visitor, English becomes increasingly established within the city, and in some *Mitte* stores one should not wonder that German is at best understood but that one should not expect to be able to fully converse in it. Economic struggle is another reason for the development of the extremely blasé attitude of the cultural establishment against the tourist seeking a distinction mechanism to slow down the redistribution of existing subsidy, donor and buyer financial capital and posts, as well as for the hedonistic class who understands that the steady influx of tourists will come at a price of a commercialization of their off-spaces and an inhibitor of their lifestyles.

*
Especially, the legendary *Bar 25*'s aesthetic of DIY wooden structures has created a lot of copycats spreading all over the city a type of adolescent playground landscape. See chapter 2.

The German language, already believed dead, becomes reestablished and popularized against the overwhelming onslaught of visitors unaccustomed to the *code* of the city. Meanwhile, for the traditional Berliners habituated to a provincial, easily affordable and protected city, tourism comes as a violent rupture throwing them into the on-setting dynamics of twenty-first century urban capitalism: rent, food and commodity prices increase: in a city with a relatively large share of inhabitants deprived of a steady economic income and to a large part unemployed, this development alters social dynamics profoundly. Hostile glances of the early morning service proletariat against those returning home mid-week from parties financed by mom and dad at the same hour. Those financially potent visitors aiming to "do" Berlin in as briefly a time as possible and provide funds from cities which boast economic structures unmatched by Berlin's reality are unconsciously ridiculing the hardship of their reality.

Tourism is therefore an infrastructure fully integrating Berlin into Europe's psycho-social division of labor. Berlin stands for psycho-active entertainment and leisure capital, the capital of soma, where disenchanted Greek and Spanish elites can travel in order to lose their political projects in a bag of MDMA at a Sunday morning sunrise outside a night club, where the constraint and hyper-disciplined Parisian bourgeois youth can find its Other and commit the transgressions which will allow it to protract psychosis of over-civilization, where Scandinavians are confronted with their maximum tolerance for chaos and gritty edge. Finally, where an Anglo-American consumer mentality can shop for stimulating summer love affairs.

$\longrightarrow$

'Division of labour'

Especially in those tourism intense summer months, visitors are shock-immersed into the heterotopias of *Neukölln* and *Friedrichshain*. After disembarking at U1's terminus *Warschauer Straße*, visitors are received by the vast-open space panorama of *Warschauer Brücke*, a festival-like setting with bands playing outside, masses of swiftly moving and to a large extent intoxicated young party people and local hippies and hipsters. Street light poles are overgrown with posters, streets are drowned with glowy eyed drug merchants, and punks are cajoling passers-by for drug-and alcohol money, while techno beats are luring them into the nearby overgrown abandoned industry aesthetics of the *RAW* space, fittingly termed "Techno-Strich" (Techno-brothel) by the locals. Almost instinctively, the visitor here becomes overwhelmed by the sensation that the seriousness of German reality is temporarily and spatially suspended, and the nearby installation projection on the *Warschauer Straße* residential block bears witness to the virtuality of the experience. Similarly, in *Kreuzkölln**, once termed to be "the epicenter of cool" by the Guardian**, in the summertime becomes populated by young alternative types along the Spree canal parallel to Neukölln's hipster artery *Weser-Straße*, bearing some of the city's most international and sophisticated gentrification.

All types of European languages or accents embedded in English can be identified along this mile-long green oasis-like strip, certain to make a long lasting impression on the visitor unused to the mixture of relaxed rural atmosphere and urban cool. Deeply embedded clichés of German aggressive

*
The space between Kreuzberg and Neukölln.

**
Berliner's tend to appropriate the terms of the big international newspapers. In an age old complex, Berlin's reality is only stabilized with its mention in the newspapers of *big brother*. In this way, the NYT's Berghain- "The Capital of Techno", or "Berlin-Silicon Allee" have had to pass by the other side of the Atlantic to become reality for Berliners themselves.

hegemonic dominance become replaced by the *soft power* attraction of the new epicenter of an emerging Neo-European spiritual empire. Tourism becomes the initiation ritual, by which international youth are introduced to the city and its nature as being the most psycho-active in the shortest possible time-span. It consequently succeeds in securing a longer-term allegiance to the city for a fraction of these highmobility classes.

PRODUCTION

Berlinification of Europe

Similar to the attraction exercised on and the brain drain towards this new European capital, Berlin also becomes an export lifestyle model through the masses exposed to the city's psycho-active formula via tourism. Berlin's cheap, internationalized, hedonistic, and thereby accessible culture becomes a readily exportable commodity for savvy entrepreneurs capable of transferring its formula to their local cultures. Alien signifiers, torn-down wallpapers, minimal beats, dressed down asceticism, pale amphetamine skin start appearing in Poznan, Hamburg, Glasgow, Ljubljana, Vienna, Warsaw, Stockholm, Toronto, soon even more resistant cultural models like Paris, Rome. Off the urban grid, they slowly infiltrate provinces marked by industrial atrophy, permanent recession, exodus.

They unite and Berlinify youth in the periphery, slowly but securely organizing networks of exfiltration...

EPILOGUE

"Paris will always be Paris but Berlin will never be Berlin". The words of former French Minister of Culture Jack Lang are emblematic for the sentiment of the rapid urban renewal processes of that shape shifting metropolis called Berlin. In the central *Unter den Linden* district the *Neue Wache** monument bears witness to the profound historical political changes that have swept the city. Originally constructed by Frederic William III for the soldiers killed in action during the Napoleonic wars, the memorial has shifted its meaning to commemorating the soldiers of WWI in 1931, to become the memorial for the victims of fascism and militarism during the socialist German Democratic Republic, and after reunification the memorial for the victims of war and dictatorship. This mnemonically promiscuous opportunistic locus has therefore been reinterpreted in every modern era of Berlin, while similarly always remaining a central ideological device of legitimacy for its current government. It epitomizes Berlin's struggle between rupture and consistency, its history of inside and outside repression, punishment, and failed attempts to emancipations: as if Berlin was always attempting to flee history in order to launch the current political project in direct opposition to the latter, to finally become caught up by the haunting images of the past again. This same character makes the city apt for displaying the most modern version of ideology and is therefore highly valuable to any analysis of the present.

* Literally "New Watch".

Meanwhile Berlin's spatial characteristics, its geopolitical, economic and strategic location give it all the potential to continue its emergence as a new player in the production of historical subjectivity in the age of aggressive capitalist expansion: Berlin after all hosts the capital of a primary vassal state in the imperial organization of space and could therefore be considered a laboratory in the production of twenty-first century state-of-the-art processes of *governance* for liberal-libertarian society. We have conducted this analysis to start mapping the manifold manifestations of what is conceived to be the freedom, alternative lifestyle and pace of Berlin. The aim of this *essai,* however, is not to criticize these infrastructures per sé or to advocate a return to some *status quo ante*. And how could we?

We ourselves are the children of these infrastructures, coined by their liberty and hardened by their nihilistic frenzy. What we seek is to observe the interaction of these "off" structures, the sectors of drugs, clubs, the arts, tourism or alternative economic models, with the inertia of contemporary economic and political reality. We observe social and psychological fragmentation, death-wish somatized social imaginaries, an advancing disorganization of logic, and the multiple technologies of allegiance to the gambles of grand capital: we suspect them to be the preconditions to *empire*.

We meanwhile acknowledge the necessity of Berlin's freedom, yet also perceive that freedom left to its own devices and without direction through powerful cultural software is bound for psychosis. Today, the result of freedom left awry is reflected in the faces of metropolitan citizens around the globe. The use of these libertarian structures therefore requires consciousness and the immune system of cultural critique which observes, wonders about, and stays present to their constantly altering operations in the formation of contemporary subjectivity.

To acknowledge this production process is to reaffirm that the world is not as it seems: that the aesthetic of Berlin is constructing an invisible normative order which we must acknowledge as an antecedent of the current reality of politics and learn to appropriate.

It will be the task of the dying species of the sociologist* to identify in detail these contemporary structures of programming. Her critique makes her the designer of historical consciousness, the creator of powerful cultural immune systems against the increasing sophistication of cybernetic power structures fueled by a near limitless desire of recording, appropriation and instrumentalization. In this world, the metropolis becomes center-stage for the contemporary *political-blackmagical*, government the continuation of the unconscious collective conduct of affairs.

*

Not necessarily as an academic, but as the conscious cognitive mapper and pattern recognizer.

Dignity in this world means remaining *estranged*, being able to guard the luxury of consciousness and thereby the divinity of decision and resistance, not abandoning destiny to the course of technology.

This analysis of the city is incomplete. It must remain an *essai* and a reminder that it is up to those who are bold enough to project their estranged vision onto those scarce city walls left untagged to change its destiny.

And not abandon the terrain of historical subjectivity to the *enemy*...

Contemporary culture has eliminated both the concept of the public and the figure of the intellectual. Former public spaces – both physical and cultural – are now either derelict or colonized by advertising. A cretinous anti-intellectualism presides, cheerled by expensively educated hacks in the pay of multinational corporations who reassure their bored readers that there is no need to rouse themselves from their interpassive stupor. The informal censorship internalized and propagated by the cultural workers of late capitalism generates a banal conformity that the propaganda chiefs of Stalinism could only ever have dreamt of imposing. Zer0 Books knows that another kind of discourse – intellectual without being academic, popular without being populist – is not only possible: it is already flourishing, in the regions beyond the striplit malls of so-called mass media and the neurotically bureaucratic halls of the academy. Zer0 is committed to the idea of publishing as a making public of the intellectual. It is convinced that in the unthinking, blandly consensual culture in which we live, critical and engaged theoretical reflection is more important than ever before.

ZERO BOOKS

Capitalist Realism Is there no alternative?
Mark Fisher
An analysis of the ways in which capitalism has presented itself as the only realistic political-economic system.
Paperback: November 27, 2009 978-1-84694-317-1 $14.95 £7.99.
eBook: July 1, 2012 978-1-78099-734-6 $9.99 £6.99.

The Wandering Who? A study of Jewish identity politics
Gilad Atzmon
An explosive unique crucial book tackling the issues of Jewish Identity Politics and ideology and their global influence.
Paperback: September 30, 2011 978-1-84694-875-6 $14.95 £8.99.
eBook: September 30, 2011 978-1-84694-876-3 $9.99 £6.99.

Clampdown Pop-cultural wars on class and gender
Rhian E. Jones
Class and gender in Britpop and after, and why 'chav' is a feminist issue.
Paperback: March 29, 2013 978-1-78099-708-7 $14.95 £9.99.
eBook: March 29, 2013 978-1-78099-707-0 $7.99 £4.99.

The Quadruple Object
Graham Harman
Uses a pack of playing cards to present Harman's metaphysical system of fourfold objects, including human access, Heidegger's indirect causation, panpsychism and ontography.
Paperback: July 29, 2011 978-1-84694-700-1 $16.95 £9.99.

Weird Realism Lovecraft and Philosophy
Graham Harman
As Hölderlin was to Martin Heidegger and Mallarmé to Jacques
Derrida, so is H.P. Lovecraft to the Speculative Realist philoso-
phers.
Paperback: September 28, 2012 978-1-78099-252-5 $24.95 £14.99.
eBook: September 28, 2012 978-1-78099-907-4 $9.99 £6.99.

Sweetening the Pill or How We Got Hooked on Hormonal Birth
Control
Holly Grigg-Spall
Is it really true? Has contraception liberated or oppressed
women?
Paperback: September 27, 2013 978-1-78099-607-3 $22.95 £12.99.
eBook: September 27, 2013 978-1-78099-608-0 $9.99 £6.99.

Why Are We The Good Guys? Reclaiming Your Mind From The
Delusions Of Propaganda
David Cromwell
A provocative challenge to the standard ideology that Western
power is a benevolent force in the world.
Paperback: September 28, 2012 978-1-78099-365-2 $26.95 £15.99.
eBook: September 28, 2012 978-1-78099-366-9 $9.99 £6.99.

The Truth about Art Reclaiming quality
Patrick Doorly
The book traces the multiple meanings of art to their various
sources, and equips the reader to choose between them.
Paperback: August 30, 2013 978-1-78099-841-1 $32.95 £19.99.

Bells and Whistles More Speculative Realism
Graham Harman
In this diverse collection of sixteen essays, lectures, and inter-
views Graham Harman lucidly explains the principles of

Speculative Realism, including his own object-oriented philosophy.
Paperback: November 29, 2013 978-1-78279-038-9 $26.95 £15.99.
eBook: November 29, 2013 978-1-78279-037-2 $9.99 £6.99.

Towards Speculative Realism: Essays and Lectures Essays and Lectures
Graham Harman
These writings chart Harman's rise from Chicago sportswriter to co founder of one of Europe's most promising philosophical movements: Speculative Realism.
Paperback: November 26, 2010 978-1-84694-394-2 $16.95 £9.99.
eBook: January 1, 1970 978-1-84694-603-5 $9.99 £6.99.

Meat Market Female flesh under capitalism
Laurie Penny
A feminist dissection of women's bodies as the fleshy fulcrum of capitalist cannibalism, whereby women are both consumers and consumed.
Paperback: April 29, 2011 978-1-84694-521-2 $12.95 £6.99.
eBook: May 21, 2012 978-1-84694-782-7 $9.99 £6.99.

Translating Anarchy The Anarchism of Occupy Wall Street
Mark Bray
An insider's account of the anarchists who ignited Occupy Wall Street.
Paperback: September 27, 2013 978-1-78279-126-3 $26.95 £15.99.
eBook: September 27, 2013 978-1-78279-125-6 $6.99 £4.99.

One Dimensional Woman
Nina Power
Exposes the dark heart of contemporary cultural life by examining pornography, consumer capitalism and the ideology of women's work.

Paperback: November 27, 2009 978-1-84694-241-9 $14.95 £7.99.
eBook: July 1, 2012 978-1-78099-737-7 $9.99 £6.99.

Dead Man Working

Carl Cederstrom, Peter Fleming

An analysis of the dead man working and the way in which capital is now colonizing life itself.

Paperback: May 25, 2012 978-1-78099-156-6 $14.95 £9.99.
eBook: June 27, 2012 978-1-78099-157-3 $9.99 £6.99.

Unpatriotic History of the Second World War

James Heartfield

The Second World War was not the Good War of legend. James Heartfield explains that both Allies and Axis powers fought for the same goals - territory, markets and natural resources.

Paperback: September 28, 2012 978-1-78099-378-2 $42.95 £23.99.
eBook: September 28, 2012 978-1-78099-379-9 $9.99 £6.99.

Find more titles at www.zero-books.net